MEETING SPACE: ONE ON ONE WITH GOD

Rev. Dr. Donna Cox

Published in 2017 in the United States by Personal Best Ministries Press/Donna cox Ministries, a subsidiary of Personal Best Ministries, LLC, 211 Stratford Lane, Xenia, Ohio 45385. Library of Congress Cataloging-in-Publications Data Cox, Donna M.

Meeting Space: One-On-One With God/Donna M. Cox
ISBN 978-0-9796955-6-8
Includes song lyrics
Includes scriptures (Holy Bible)
Includes art

Summary:A prayer and reflection journal

a 2017 publication of
Donna Cox Ministries/PBM Press
a subsidiary of

Personal Best
M I N I S T R I E S
LLC

MEETING SPACE

DONNA M. COX

This journal is dedicated to:

- God, the creator of music and the giver of every good and perfect gift;
- Jesus, the best storyteller, who loved me enough to offer Himself as a sacrifice for me;
- Holy Spirit who guides, instructs, comforts and enables me to offer my gifts back to The Creator and
- my daughter-in-love, Charissa Perez Cox, who is the inspiration for this journal. Thank you for allowing space in your heart for another mother.

With Gratitude I thank God for:

- Jetsly for her ability to format the journal sections to my vision;
- Zaheera for the beautiful mandalas;
- Susan K. Smith and Gene Cantadino for the beautiful prayers;
- a family filled with gifts just waiting to ripen. Seriously, y'all, 'eye has not seen; ear has not heard; neither has it entered into the imagination all that God has planned' for you. And of course, 'to whom much is given, much is required.' I'm just saying!
- pushing me well beyond my comfort zone, for insisting that I not put myself in a box of others' or my own design, that I see the creativity You've given as prophetic gifts for such a time as this and
- every person who will accept the invitation to the meeting and take the One-On-One journey.

USING THE JOURNAL

Now to Him who is able to do exceedingly abundantly above all that we ask or think, according to the power that works in us. Ephesians 3: 20 (WEB)

MEETING SPACE

noun:

a place set aside for people to get together

a place where issues are discussed, priorities set and decisions made

Meeting Space: One-On-One With God is a sacred place where a team member (journaler) meets with the CEO (God) for one-on-one, private exchanges. Meeting Space provides multiple formats for these meetings. Brief explanations and suggestions as well as a sample for each of the formats follow. Journalers should feel free to personalize any of these suggested formats to suit her own needs.

Coaching Session

Coaching is a useful way to develop skills, enhance growth potential and deal with issues, challenges or for futures planning. Meeting Space offers journalers space to experience coaching utilizing three important voices:

  • LYRICS FROM CONTEMPORARY SECULAR SONG. Music is an amazing tool for transformation. Typically, this belief is applied to the harmonic, melodic and rhythmic structures. However, song texts are a rich fount of inspiration and transformation, drawing listeners and singers into reflection on the conditions of life, its struggles and joys. Drawn from a survey in which participants were asked to identify songs that inspire them, journalers are invited to locate their own revelation in the provided texts.

  • PASSAGES OF HOLY SCRIPTURE. Each song lyric selection is paired with a Biblical text with a similar message or theme. Journalers are encouraged to reflect deeply upon these passages, listening for God's voice.

  • THE JOURNALER'S OWN WISDOM. A prompt, drawn from the song lyrics and scripture passage, asks the journaler to move beyond the initial inspiration to an internal place of enlightenment, growth and action. The very act of putting pen to paper invites the journaler to explore her own hidden, forgotten or untapped wisdom.

Extend the coaching page by listening to a recording of the song. Read the scripture in context of the chapter.

Here's a little song I wrote. You might want to sing it note for note. Don't worry; be happy. In every life we have some trouble. But when you worry, you make it double. Don't worry; be happy. Don't Worry, Be Happy (Bobby McFerrin)

Don't worry about anything; instead, pray about everything; tell God your needs, and don't forget to thank him for his answers. If you do this, you will experience God's peace, which is far more wonderful than the human mind can understand. His peace will keep your thoughts and your hearts quiet and at rest as you trust in Christ Jesus.
Philippians 4: 6-7 (TLB)

Journaling Prompt:
I worry too much about _____.
I need peace in my _____.

5-16-17

I worry too much about what
other people think about me! Lord,
I need peace in my mind. My
thoughts circle around like mice
on a treadmill — or whatever you
call it! Bobby McFerrin makes it
seem so simple — and I guess at
the end of the day it is. The
scripture says "don't worry"! That
must mean that I have a choice.
Today, I choose to not worry about
anything. When the thoughts
start to circle I'll pray! I
need peace!! I NEED PEACE!!
I NEED PEACE! And I get
to choose peace. I get to choose
where my thoughts go! Today,
just for today, one minute at
a time I choose to tell my
thoughts to shut up and
I will look for ways to
experience peace!!

Today is a great day to
experience God's peace!!

PRAYING FORWARD

Jesus grew in wisdom and in stature and in favor with God and all people. Luke 2:52: (NLT)

Using Jesus as a model, this page invited journalers to consider practical ways to apply what they've been discovering through the coaching pages.

As you move through the coaching pages, you will be drawn to specific ways to:

- feed your soul
    (favor with God);
- feed your mind
    (knowledge and wisdom);
- feed your body
    (stature) and
- feed others
    (favor with all people).

Praying Forward 5/17/16

FEED MY SOUL

Meditate on Phil 4:6-7
Don't worry; PRAY ABOUT EVERYTHING even the little stuff coz God cares

FEED MY MIND

Read Parker Palmer's book, Let Your Life Speak

FEED MY BODY

This week -
• Reduce sugar
• Move! Make sure I get 10000 steps in at least 5 days!

FEED OTHERS

Reach out to Cindy. She's looked sad to me.
May do lunch or take a walk?

Remember, the journey is never simply about personal growth. Being fully alive and whole gives us the pleasure and privilege of using what we know about ourselves and God to make the world a better place.

MEETING WITH THE CEO

These pages invite the journaler to consider, more deeply, a passage from the coaching sessions or a verse that may have come up during reflection. Write the scripture, either directly from the Bible or in your own words, in the provided space. In the next space, write the main idea or the point that speaks most clearly to you. Then consider practical action steps for using what you received from the scripture. Write at least one step and commit to following through.

Studying scripture is so much fun! If you are new to the discipline, consider using the Blue Letter Bible. It will give you a chance to do word searches or read a variety of commentaries. The goal for the meetings is always about application of what you learn!

DOODLES TO CLARITY

Use these pages to tap into your inner creative while God speaks to you. There is no right or wrong way to do this and you do not have to be 'an artist.' In fact, you probably doodled quite a bit before you 'grew up.' Did you know that doodling has been linked to improved memory, cognitive functioning and even stress reduction? Consider drawing shapes, illustrations, words or simply give your pencil or pen permission to move about the page as you reflect on a question for which you seek clarity, a concept or a passage of scripture. Do not 'grade' yourself. This activity will not be used for a performance or merit evaluation. As you give yourself permission to simply fill your page, you may very well find answers - or healing.

Doodles to
Clarity

Hebrews 4:12 The Word of God penetrates, dividing soul & spirit, joints & marrow; it judges the thoughts and attitudes of the heart

PEOPLE IN 3 parts like God (God Jesus HS)

SPIRIT
SOUL = MIND, WILL, EMOTIONS
BODY
WORD OF GOD
The temple
Gotta exercise
The Real Me!!
God Judges
How do I take care of all?
How I Show up IN THE WORLD

MANDALAS

Meeting Space includes ten mandalas with scripture passages. Enjoy coloring these pages as you reflect. The back page is empty so you can be confident using markers and pens. You might also choose to use the back page as an additional page for journaling.

BULLET PRAYERS

In the morning, O LORD, you hear my voice;
in the morning I lay my requests before you and wait in expectation. Psalm 5:3.

Maintaining a prayer journal is a wonderful way to focus time spent in conversation with God. However, many people are intimidated by the process. Bullet prayers provide a wonderful introduction to keeping a record of your prayer requests AND ways God moves. They are not as in-depth, detailed or florid as a traditional prayer journal and do not require a major investment of time.

In these pages, write 'quick prayers' or note the broad strokes of a specific concern in the prayer column.

From time to time, review your bullet prayers and make a notation in the update column.

PRAYERS	UPDATES
5/10 • Charlie needs a job-like now	5/30-He got call !!
• Marianne's surgery	all went well.
• My 12:00 test. I Studied but I still feel anxious	I ACED IT !!
• Joann & Phil are considering divorce. Intervene, Lord!	9/15-started counseling. ☺
• Lauren's party to be great!	
5/12 • Heal Mom's eyes quickly. The surgery went well.	
• Anya's college tours.	
• My weight & attitude about food - Scream!	9/1 Lost 2 lbs
• Guam! God help !!	
5/20 • Flooding in Texas. How can I help ?	5/23 Our home group is collecting $
• Melody is having the baby today! Pray for safety.	Healthy baby boy. No meds !!
6/3 • Julia's grandmother died. Heal her family's ♡	
• My art work to be well-received	7/5 The exhibit was fantastic

Count your blessings; name them one by one,
Count your blessings; see what God has done!
Count your blessings; name them one by one,
And it will surprise you what the Lord has done!
Count Your Blessings, Jason Oatman, Jr.

The name of the Lord is a strong tower;
the righteous run into it and are safe. Proverbs 18:10

Charm is deceitful and beauty is vain, but a woman who fears the Lord is to be praised. Proverbs 31:30

SECTIONS ONE & TWO

COLORFUL MUSICAL PRAYERS

Each day, we search, O God,
and attune our ear to the different melodies
that surround us. Above all, we desire a place
where our disparate voices can be joined
into a harmony which will reveal
Your kin[g]dom symphony.
Guide us with Your wisdom so that
we will know how to add our song to
those of our contemporaries and
thus, as a people, we will recreate
the face of the earth today and forever

Fr. Gene Cantadino
Used by permission

I'm not the average girl from your video. And I ain't built like a supermodel. But I learned to love myself unconditionally because I am a queen. When I look in the mirror and the only one there is me, every freckle on my face is where it's suppose to be. And I know my creator didn't make no mistakes on me. My feet, my thighs, my lips, my eyes; I'm loving what I see.
Video/Average Girl (India Arie)

You made all the delicate, inner parts of my body and knit me together in my mother's womb. Thank you for making me so wonderfully complex! Your workmanship is marvelous— how well I know it.
Psalm 139: 13-18 (TLB)

Journaling Prompt:
Lord, help me to love my
_____ unconditionally.

Sometimes it feels like I'll never go past here. Sometimes it feels like I'm stuck forever and ever. But, I'm going higher, closer to my dreams. I'm goin' higher and higher; I can almost reach. Some times you just have to let it go, leaving all my fears to burn down, push them all away so I can move on, closer to my dreams. Feel it all over my being, close your eyes and see what you believe. Closer (Goapele)

Put GOD in charge of your work, then what you've planned will take place
Proverbs 16:3 (MSG))

Journaling Prompt:
Lord, give me courage to move closer to this dream.

From the day we arrive on the planet, and blinking, step into the sun, there's more to be seen than can ever be seen, more to do than can ever be done. Some say eat or be eaten. Some say live and let live. But all are agreed as they join the stampede, you should never take more than you give in the circle of life.
Circle Of Life (Elton John)

Remember this, whoever sows sparingly will also reap sparingly and whoever sows bountifully will also reap bountifully. 2 Corinthians 9:6 (NIV)

Journaling Prompt:
Lord, in what area of my life do I need to practice generosity?

This ain't a song for the broken-hearted; no silent prayer for the faith-departed. I ain't gonna be just a face in the crowd . You're gonna hear my voice when I shout it out loud. It's my life. It's now or never; I ain't gonna live forever. I just want to live while I'm alive.

It's My Life (Bon Jovi)

The thief comes only in order to steal and kill and destroy. I came that they may have and enjoy life, and have it in abundance [to the full, till it overflows]. John 10:10 (AMP)

Journaling Prompt:

I have allowed the thief to steal _____.

Today, I start the journey of

reclaiming _____.

Here's a little song I wrote. You might want to sing it note for note. Don't worry; be happy. In every life we have some trouble. But when you worry, you make it double. Don't worry; be happy. Don't Worry, Be Happy (Bobby McFerrin)

Don't worry about anything; instead, pray about everything; tell God your needs, and don't forget to thank him for his answers. If you do this, you will experience God's peace, which is far more wonderful than the human mind can understand. His peace will keep your thoughts and your hearts quiet and at rest as you trust in Christ Jesus.
Philippians 4: 6-7 (TLB)

Journaling Prompt:
I worry too much about _____.
I need peace in my _____.

_____
_____
_____
_____
_____
_____
_____
_____
_____
_____
_____
_____
_____
_____
_____
_____
_____
_____
_____
_____
_____
_____
_____
_____
_____
_____
_____
_____
_____
_____

Praying
Forward

FEED MY SOUL

FEED MY MIND

FEED MY BODY

FEED OTHERS

Meeting with the CEO

SCRIPTURE PASSAGE	MAIN IDEAS

ACTION ITEMS

meeting with the CEO

SCRIPTURE PASSAGE	MAIN IDEAS

ACTION ITEMS

Doodles to

Clarity

Doodles to Clarity

DON'T BE ANXIOUS ABOUT ANYTHING, BUT IN EVERY SITUATION, BY PRAYER AND PETITION, WITH THANKSGIVING, PRESENT YOUR REQUESTS TO GOD PHIL 4:6

Don't be anxious about anything, but in every situation, by prayer and petition, with thanksgiving, present your requests to God. Philippians 4:6

I am beautiful. No matter what they say, words can't bring me down. I am beautiful in every single way. No matter what we do; no matter what we say; we're the song inside the tune, full of beautiful mistakes. And everywhere we go the sun will always shine.
Beautiful (Christina Aguilera)

You are altogether beautiful, my darling; there is no flaw in you.
Song of Solomon 4:7 (NIV)

Journaling Prompt:
I'm beautiful! My _____ is not a flaw and I will no longer ___.

_____
_____
_____
_____
_____
_____
_____
_____
_____
_____
_____
_____
_____
_____
_____
_____
_____
_____
_____
_____
_____
_____
_____
_____
_____
_____
_____
_____
_____
_____

We are the champions, my friends. And we'll keep on fighting 'til the end. We are the champions. No time for losers 'cause we are the champions of the world.
We Are the Champions (Queen)

No, in all these things we are more than conquerors through him who loved us.
Romans 8:37 (NIV))

Journaling Prompt:
I am a winner! I believe I can _____.

_____
_____
_____
_____
_____
_____
_____
_____
_____
_____
_____
_____
_____
_____
_____
_____
_____
_____
_____
_____
_____
_____
_____
_____
_____
_____
_____
_____
_____
_____

First, when there's nothing but a slow glowing dream that your fear seems to hide deep inside your mind. All alone, I have cried silent tears full of pride. In a world made of steel, made of stone, I hear the music, close my eyes, feel the rhythm. Wrap around; take a hold of my heart. What a feeling; being's believing. I can have it all, now I'm dancing for my life. Take your passion and make it happen. Pictures come alive. You can dance right through your life.
Flashdance… What A Feeling (Irene Cara)

We also pray that you will be strengthened with all His glorious power so you will have all the endurance and patience you need. May you be filled with joy.
Colossians 1:11 (NLT)

Journaling Prompt:
I want to be filled with joy.
God, make me stronger in _____.

When I wake up in the morning, and the sunlight hurts my eyes, and something without warning bears heavy on my mind. Then I look at you and the world's alright with me. Just one look at you and I know it's gonna be a lovely day.When the day that lies ahead of me seems impossible to face. When someone else instead of me always seems to know the way, then I look at you and the world's alright with me. Just one look at you and I know it's gonna be a lovely day.
Lovely Day (Bill Withers)

This is the very day GOD acted. Let's celebrate and be festive. Psalm 118:24 (MSG)

Journaling Prompt: What an amazing day. I choose to celebrate ___.

I see trees of green, red roses too. I see them bloom for me and you. And I think to myself what \a wonderful world. I see skies of blue and clouds of white. The bright blessed day, the dark sacred night. And I think to myself what a wonderful world.
What A Wonderful World (Louis Armstrong)

What a wildly, wonderful world God made! You made it all with wisdom at your side, made earth overflow with your wonderful creations. Psalm 104:24 (MSG)

Journaling Prompt:
When I look at _____
I see evidence of your____, God.

Praying Forward

FEED MY SOUL

FEED MY MIND

FEED MY BODY

FEED OTHERS

Meeting with the CEO

SCRIPTURE PASSAGE	MAIN IDEAS

ACTION ITEMS

Meeting with the CEO

SCRIPTURE PASSAGE

MAIN IDEAS

ACTION ITEMS

Doodles to Clarity

TRUST IN THE LORD WITH ALL YOUR HEART AND DO NOT LEAN ON YOUR OWN UNDERSTANDING PROV 3:5 ♥

Proverbs 3:5 Trust in the Lord with all your heart and do not lean on your own understanding.

SECTIONS THREE & FOUR

COLORFUL MUSICAL PRAYERS

I look up to the hills.
I look to friends, family, doctors, my intellect;
where does my help come from?
It's not in any of my humanly resources.
My help comes from the Lord, the maker of
Heaven and earth, the Creator!
My Lord will never let me be defeated.
My guard is on duty 24/7, never drifts to sleep
or takes a potty break.
As the mountains, strong, majestic,
natural fortresses, surround Jerusalem,
the Lord surrounds me, now and forever!
You are my help!
Because of your protection, I sing.
My help comes from the Lord
who made Heaven, earth and me.

Rev. Donna M. Cox
based on Psalm 121:1-2

It's funny how some distance makes everything seem small. And the fears that once controlled me, can't get to me at all. It's time to see what I can do, to test the limits and break through.
Let It Go (Idina Menzel)

For God has not given us a spirit of fear and timidity, but of power, love, and self-discipline.
2 Timothy 1:7 (NIV)

Journaling Prompt:
God, You give me power even when I feel weak.
Today, I take a healing breath of courage and _____.

_____
_____
_____
_____
_____
_____
_____
_____
_____
_____
_____
_____
_____
_____
_____
_____
_____
_____
_____
_____
_____
_____
_____
_____
_____
_____
_____
_____
_____
_____
_____

I am a mountain. I am a tall tree. I am a swift wind sweeping the country. I am a river down in the valley. I am a vision and I can see clearly. If anybody asks you who I am, just stand up tall, look 'em in the face and say I'm that star up in the sky. I'm that mountain peak up high. I'm the world's greatest. I'm that little bit of hope when my back's against the ropes. I can feel it. I'm the world's greatest.
The World's Greatest (R. Kelly)

But those who hope in the Lord will renew their strength. They will soar on wings like eagles; they will run and not grow weary, they will walk and not be faint.
Isaiah 40:31 (NIV)

Journaling Prompt:
Today, Lord, I see myself as....

_____
_____
_____
_____
_____
_____
_____
_____
_____
_____
_____
_____
_____
_____
_____
_____
_____
_____
_____
_____
_____
_____
_____
_____
_____
_____
_____
_____
_____
_____
_____
_____
_____

I used to think that I could not go on and life was nothing but an awful song. But now I know the meaning of true love. I'm leaning on the everlasting arms. If I can see it, then I can do it. If I just believe it, there's nothing to it. I believe I can fly. I believe I can touch the sky. I think about it every night and day, spread my wings and fly away. I believe I can soar. I see me running through that open door. I believe I can fly. I Believe I Can Fly (R. Kelly)

I can do all things through Christ who strengthens me.
Philippians 4:13 (NKJV))

Journaling Prompt:
I have always wanted to _____.
This is what it might look like
if I just take a chance.

_____
_____
_____
_____
_____
_____
_____
_____
_____
_____
_____
_____
_____
_____
_____
_____
_____
_____
_____
_____
_____
_____
_____
_____
_____
_____
_____
_____
_____
_____
_____
_____

It's a beautiful morning I think I'll go outside a
while and just smile, just take in some clean fresh
air. Ain't no sense in stayin' inside if the weather's
fine, and you got the time. It's your chance to
wake up and plan another brand new day.
Either way, it's a beautiful morning, each
bird keeps singing his own song.
 A Beautiful Morning (The Rascals)

The LORD'S loving kindnesses indeed
never cease, For His compassions
never fails. They are new every
morning; Great is Your faithfulness.
Lamentations 3: 22-23 (NASB))

Journaling Prompt:
It is a new day, with new promises
and possibilities. Today, I choose _____.

When I look around I see blue skies. I see butterflies for us Listen to the sound and lose it. Its sweet music and dance with me. There is beauty in the world, so much beauty in the world. Always beauty in the world, so much beauty in the world. Beauty In The World (Macy Gray)

Let the heavens rejoice, let the earth be glad; let the sea resound, and all that is in it. Let the fields be jubilant, and everything in them; let all the trees of the forest sing for joy.
Psalm 96:11-12 (NIV)

Journaling Prompt:
Look around. Describe the beauty that surrounds you.

_____
_____
_____
_____
_____
_____
_____
_____
_____
_____
_____
_____
_____
_____
_____
_____
_____
_____
_____
_____
_____
_____
_____
_____
_____
_____
_____
_____
_____
_____

Praying Forward

FEED MY SOUL

FEED MY MIND

FEED MY BODY

FEED OTHERS

Meeting with the CEO

SCRIPTURE PASSAGE

MAIN IDEAS

ACTION ITEMS

Meeting with the CEO

SCRIPTURE PASSAGE

MAIN IDEAS

ACTION ITEMS

Doodles to Clarity

THE LORD IS MY SHEPHERD, I LACK NOTHING PS 23:1

The Lord is my Shepherd, I lack nothing.
Psalm 23:1

From a distance we all have enough and no one is in need. There are no guns, no bombs and no disease, no hungry mouths to feed. From a distance we are instruments marching in a common band, playing songs of hope, playing songs of peace. They are the songs of every man. God is watching us.
From A Distance (Bette Midler)

For I was hungry and you gave me something to eat. I was thirsty and you gave me something to drink. I was a stranger and you invited me in. I needed clothes and you clothed me. I was sick and you looked after me. I was in prison and you came to visit me.
Matthew 25:35-40 (NIV))

Journaling Prompt:
Lord, who do you want me to SEE today and how should I respond?

_____
_____
_____
_____
_____
_____
_____
_____
_____
_____
_____
_____
_____
_____
_____
_____
_____
_____
_____
_____
_____
_____
_____
_____
_____
_____
_____

I can see laughter, or I can see tears. I see a choice, love or fear. What do you choose? I can see peace, or I can see war. I can see sunshine, or I can see a storm. What do you choose? Now I choose to live with freedom flying from my heart, where the light keeps shining. I choose to feel the whole world crying for the strength that we can rise above. I choose Love.
I Choose Love (Shawn Gallaway)

And now, dear brothers and sisters, one final thing. Fix your thoughts on what is true, and honorable, and right, and pure, and lovely, and admirable. Think about things that are excellent and worthy of praise.
Philippians 4:8 (NLT)

Journaling Prompt:
In what ways do you need to fix your thoughts? Choose one to write and pray about.

What would you think if I sang out of tune?
Would you stand up and walk out on me?
Lend me your ears and I'll sing you a song.
And I'll try not to sing out of key. I get by with
a little help from my friends.
With a Little Help From My Friends (Beatles)

Two are better off than one, because
together they can work more effectively.
Ecclesiastes 4:9 (NLT)

Journaling Prompt:
Give thanks for a friend for whom
you are grateful. Considering taking
it a step farther and sending a
handwritten note.

That's not the beginning of the end. That's the return to yourself, the return to innocence. Love devotion; feeling emotion. Don't be afraid to be weak. Don't be too proud to be strong. Just look into your heart, my friend. That will be the return to yourself, the return to innocence. If you want, then start to laugh. If you must, then start to cry. Be yourself don't hide. Just believe in destiny.

Return To Innocence (Enigma)

But GOD told Samuel, "Looks aren't everything. Don't be impressed with his looks and stature. I've already eliminated him. GOD judges persons differently than humans do. Men and women look at the face; GOD looks into the heart."

1 Samuel 16:7 (MSG)

Journaling Prompt:
How is your heart? In what ways do you judge yourself?
How can you offer yourself more grace?

Do you ever feel like a plastic bag, drifting through the wind, wanting to start again? Do you ever feel so paper thin, like a house of cards, one blow from caving in? Do you ever feel already buried deep, six feet under; screams but no one seems to hear a thing? Do you know that there's still a chance for you because there's a spark in you. You just gotta ignite the light, and let it shine. Just own the night like the 4th of July because you're a firework.
Firework (Katy Perry)

For this reason, I remind you to fan into flame the gift of God which is in you through the laying on of my hands.
2 Timothy 1:6 (NIV)

Journaling Prompt:
Lord, what gift do I need to rekindle or set on fire?

Praying Forward

FEED MY SOUL

FEED MY MIND

FEED MY BODY

FEED OTHERS

Meeting with the CEO

SCRIPTURE PASSAGE

MAIN IDEAS

ACTION ITEMS

Meeting with the CEO

SCRIPTURE PASSAGE	MAIN IDEAS

ACTION ITEMS

_____
_____
_____
_____
_____
_____
_____
_____
_____
_____
_____
_____
_____
_____
_____
_____
_____
_____

Doodles to Clarity

God gives strength to the weary and increases the power of the weak. Isaiah 40:29

Sections Five & Six

COLORFUL MUSICAL PRAYERS

I will lie down and sleep in peace for you,
O Lord, make me dwell in safety. Psalm 4:8

Mother, there's too many of you crying. Brother, there's far too many of you dying. You know we've got to find a way to bring some lovin' here today. Father, we don't need to escalate. You see, war is not the answer for only love can conquer hate. You know we've got to find a way to bring some lovin' here today. Picket lines and picket signs; don't punish me with brutality. Talk to me, so you can see what's going on? What's Going On (Marvin Gaye)

Don't let evil conquer you, but conquer evil by doing good.
Romans 12:21 (NIV)

Journaling Prompt: How good can you do in the face of evil? What do you need from God?

_____
_____
_____
_____
_____
_____
_____
_____
_____
_____
_____
_____
_____
_____
_____
_____
_____
_____
_____
_____
_____
_____
_____
_____
_____
_____
_____
_____
_____
_____

Hello fear, before you sit down there's something I need to explain. Since you're here, I think I should tell you, since we last talked things have changed. See, I'm tired of being broken-hearted so I made a list and you're on it. All my hopes and my dreams, you took from me. I want those back before you leave. Never again will I love you. My heart refuses to be your home. No longer your prisoner, today I remember, apart from you is where I belong. And never again will I trust you. 'm tired of fighting; it's been way too long. No longer your prisoner, today I remember, who I was and now it's gone. Hello Fear (Kirk Franklin)

I prayed to the Lord, and he answered me. He freed me from all my fears.

Psalm 34:4 (ESV)

Journaling Prompt: Write to your fear and let God reveal your inner strength.

I've been a victim of a selfish kind of love. It's time that I realize that there are some with no home, not a nickel to loan. Could it be really me, pretending that they're not alone? A willow deeply scarred, somebody's broken heart and a washed-out dream. They follow the pattern on the wind, ya' see 'Cause they got no place to be That's why I'm starting with me. I'm starting with the man in the mirror. I'm asking him to change his ways. No message could have been any clearer; if you want to make the world a better place, take a look at yourself and make a change.
Man In The Mirror (Michael Jackson)

For if you give, you will get! Your gift will return to you in full and overflowing measure, pressed down, shaken together to make room for more, and running over. Whatever measure you use to give— large or small—will be used to measure what is given back to you.
Luke 6:38 (TLB)

Journaling Prompt: When I look at myself in the mirror I see.....

It might seem crazy what I'm about to say. Sunshine, she's here, you can take away. I'm a hot air balloon. I could go to space with the air, like I don't care, because I'm happy. Clap along if you feel like a room without a roof. Clap along if you feel like happiness is the truth. Clap along if you know what happiness is to you. Clap along if you feel like that's what you wanna do.... Here's why. Because I'm happy.
Happy (Pharrell Williams)

Rejoice in the Lord always; again I will say, Rejoice.
Philippians 4:4 (ESV)

Journaling Prompt:
When I think about ____ I feel like dancing!

You were my strength when I was weak. You were my voice when I couldn't speak. You were my eyes when I couldn't see. You saw the best there was in me. Lifted me up when I couldn't reach, You gave me faith 'coz you believed. I'm everything I am because you loved me. Because You Loved Me (Celine Dion)

Indeed, I have inscribed a picture of you on the palms of My hands.
Isaiah 49:16a (AMP)

Journaling Prompt:
When have you felt God lift you when you did not think you could move?

Praying
Forward

FEED MY SOUL

FEED MY MIND

FEED MY BODY

FEED OTHERS

Meeting with the CEO

SCRIPTURE PASSAGE

MAIN IDEAS

ACTION ITEMS

Meeting with the CEO

SCRIPTURE PASSAGE	MAIN IDEAS

ACTION ITEMS

Doodles to Clarity

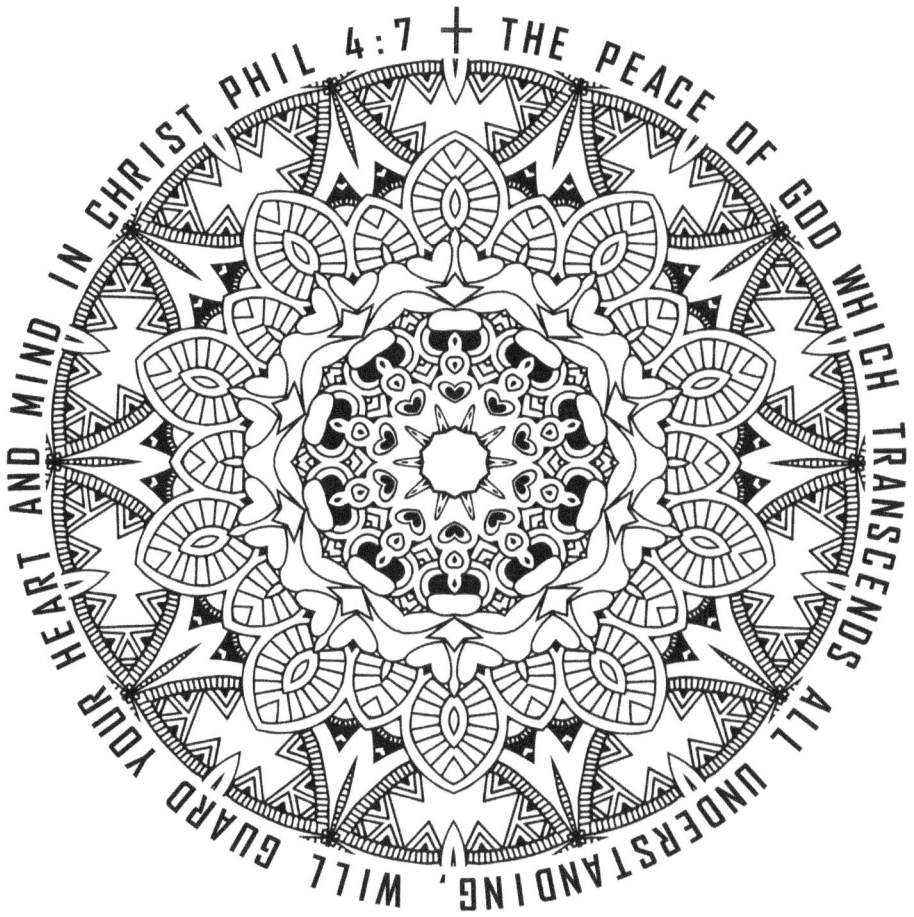

The peace of God which transcends all understanding, will guard your heart and mind in Christ. Philippians 4:7

No matter how hard reality seems, just hold on to your dreams. Don't give up and don't give, in although it seems you never win. You will always pass the test as long as you keep your head to the sky. You can win as long as you keep your head to the sky.
Optimistic (Sounds of Blackness)

Trust in the Lord with all your heart, and do not rely on your own understanding; think about Him in all your ways, and He will guide you on the right paths.
Proverbs 3:5-6 (HCSB)

Journaling Prompt:
God, I do not understand ___. I turn to you for direction. Help me ___.

_____
_____
_____
_____
_____
_____
_____
_____
_____
_____
_____
_____
_____
_____
_____
_____
_____
_____
_____
_____
_____
_____
_____
_____
_____
_____
_____
_____
_____
_____
_____

Everyday is a new day. I'm thankful for every breath I take. I won't take it for granted so I learn from my mistakes. It's beyond my control. Sometimes it's best to let go, whatever happens in this lifetime. So I trust in love. You have given me peace of mind. I feel so alive for the very first time. I can't deny you. I feel so alive for the very first time. And I think I can fly.
Alive (P.O.D.)

He will keep in perfect peace all those who trust in him, whose thoughts turn often to the Lord!
Isaiah 26: 3 (TLB)

Journaling Prompt:
What thought continually robs you of peace? How can you give it to God and refocus for peace?

I pray You'll be our eyes and watch us where we go. And help us to be wise in times when we don't know. Let this be our prayer when we lose our way. Lead us to the place. Guide us with Your grace to a place where we'll be safe.
The Prayer (Celine Dion)

You are my hiding place; you will protect me from trouble and surround me with songs of deliverance.
Psalm 32:7 (NIV)

Journaling Prompt:
I feel ___ today. Hide me while I ____. Fill me with _____.

Standing here in Your presence, in a grace so relentless, I am won by perfect love, wrapped within the arms of heaven in a peace that lasts forever. Sinking deep in mercy's sea I'm wide awake. Drawing close, stirred by grace and all my heart is Yours. All fear removed, I breathe You in. I lean into Your love. When I'm lost You pursue me, lift my head to see Your glory. Lord of all, so beautiful, here in You I find shelter. [I am] captivated by the splendor of Your face, my secret place.
Sinking Deep (Hillsong Young & Free)

You, O Lord, will not withhold Your compassion from me; Your lovingkindness and Your truth will continually preserve me.
Psalm 40:11 (NAS)

Journaling Prompt:
Choose a quote from the song lyrics to reflect upon.

You shout it out but I can't hear a word you say. I'm talking loud, not saying much. I'm criticized but all your bullets ricochet. You shoot me down, but I get up. I'm bulletproof, nothing to lose. Fire away. Ricochet. You take your aim. Fire away. You shoot me down but I won't fall. I am titanium.
Titanium (David Guetta)

Be strong and courageous. Do not be afraid or terrified because of them, for the LORD your God goes with you; He will never leave you nor forsake you.
Deuteronomy 31:6 (NIV)

Journaling Prompt:
Draw and image of yourself in a bubble. A stick figure is perfect. Write the things that are ricocheting off you. Give thanks!

Praying Forward

FEED MY SOUL

FEED MY MIND

FEED MY BODY

FEED OTHERS

Meeting with the CEO

SCRIPTURE PASSAGE

MAIN IDEAS

ACTION ITEMS

Meeting with the CEO

SCRIPTURE PASSAGE

MAIN IDEAS

ACTION ITEMS

Doodles to Clarity

THE SPIRIT OF GOD GAVE US DOES NOT MAKE US TIMID, BUT GIVES US POWER, LOVE AND SELF-DISCIPLINE 2TIM 1:7 ♥

The spirit God gave us does not make us timid, but gives us power, love and self-discipline. 2 Timothy 1:7

Sections SEVEN & EIGHT

COLORFUL MUSICAL PRAYERS

God who waits ...we thank You.
You wait for us to stop wallowing,
to stop mourning and stop looking at all the reasons
we cannot do what You have gifted us to do.
You wait for us to listen to and for Your voice,
to hear the blessed assurance and to feel the gentle
nudges You give us to move from fear to faith.
You wait for us to jump off the ledges on which we stand
and realize that we are not wingless birds but are instead
eagles, with huge wingspans, able to traverse the realm of
possibility and opportunity which You have placed before us.
You wait for us to take the first leap, to close our eyes
and just ...jump ...trusting that You are there and that
You won't even have to catch us
because You equipped us to fly.
On this day, help us not to stand looking down
and therefore not able to feel Your spirit hovering over us,
but help us to look up and to dare lift our wings
...just a bit ...and feel the spirit of You make those
wings expand and take us up and forward.
You have been waiting;
You will not wait forever.
On the ledge, You wait with us.
Help us to trust that ...and to jump. Amen.

Rev. Susan K. Smith
Used with permission

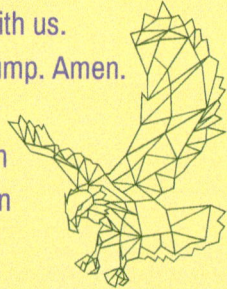

She just wants to be beautiful. She goes unnoticed. She knows no limits. She craves attention. She praises an image. She prays to be sculpted by the sculptor. She doesn't see the light that's shining deeper than the eyes can find. Maybe we have made her blind so she tries to cover up her pain, and cut her woes away because cover girls don't cry after their face is made. But there's a hope that's waiting for you in the dark. You should know you're beautiful just the way you are and you don't have to change a thing. The world could change its heart. No scars to your beautiful.
Scars To Your Beautiful (Alessia Cara)

Your beauty should not come from outward adornment, such as elaborate hairstyles and the wearing of gold jewelry or fine clothes. Rather, it should be that of your inner self, the unfading beauty of a gentle and quiet spirit, which is of great worth in God's sight.
1 Peter 3:3-4 (NIV)

Journaling Prompt:
You are precious! What part of your inner self have you ignored or allowed others to diminish? Write about it, celebrate it and give thanks.

_____
_____
_____
_____
_____
_____
_____
_____
_____
_____
_____
_____
_____
_____
_____
_____
_____
_____
_____
_____
_____
_____
_____
_____
_____

I hope you never lose your sense of wonder. You get your fill to eat but always keep that hunger. May you never take one single breath for granted. God forbid, love ever leave you empty-handed. I hope you still feel small when you stand beside the ocean. Whenever one door closes I hope one more opens. Promise me that you'll give faith a fighting chance. And when you get the choice to sit it out or dance, I hope you dance.
I Hope You Dance (Lee Ann Womack)

Now you've got my feet on the life path, all radiant from the shining of your face. Ever since you took my hand, I'm on the right way..
Psalm 16:11 (MSG)

Journaling Prompt:
Which line of the song lyrics speaks to you? Are you on the path to choosing to dance?

_____
_____
_____
_____
_____
_____
_____
_____
_____
_____
_____
_____
_____
_____
_____
_____
_____
_____
_____
_____
_____
_____
_____
_____
_____
_____
_____
_____
_____
_____
_____

Today's a new day, but there is no sunshine, nothing but clouds, and it's dark in my heart. And it feels like a cold night. Today's a new day. Where are my blue skies? Where is the love and the joy that you promised me? I almost gave up, but a power that I can't explain fell from heaven like a shower. I smile. Even though I hurt I smile. I know God is working so I smile. Even though I've been here for a while, I smile.
I Smile (Kirk Franklin)

And we know that God causes everything to work together for the good of those who love God and are called according to his purpose for them.
Romans 8:28 (NLT)

Journaling Prompt:
What clouds seem to be covering your 'blue skies?' How might God be knitting them together for your good?

I am exactly where I need to be. I need to be exactly where I am. I am a blessing manifest and I can undress the moment. Naked time unwinds beneath my mind and, from within, I find the kind of beauty only I can find. I am surrendering so willingly to be the perfect me inside this now. And truly, how else could it be? Exactly (Amy Steinberg)

For I am confident of this very thing, that He who began a good work in you will perfect it until the day of Christ Jesus.
Philippians 1:6 (NASB)

Journaling Prompt:
You are where you are for a reason.
What can you do to stop fighting
the revelation of your purpose?

Hope when you take that jump, you don't fear the fall. Hope when the water rises, you built a wall. Hope when the crowd screams out, they're screaming your name. Hope if everybody runs, you choose to stay. Hope that you fall in love, and it hurts so bad. The only way you can know is give it all you have. Lived (One Republic)

Whatever you do, do it enthusiastically, as something done for the Lord...
Colossians 3:23 (CEV)

Journaling Prompt:
Write about a job or task you have to do but do not really like. How can you shift your focus from dislike to enthusiasm?

Praying Forward

| FEED MY SOUL | FEED MY MIND |

| FEED MY BODY | FEED OTHERS |

Meeting with the CEO

SCRIPTURE PASSAGE

MAIN IDEAS

ACTION ITEMS

Meeting with the CEO

SCRIPTURE PASSAGE	MAIN IDEAS

ACTION ITEMS

Doodles to *Clarity*

Doodles to Clarity

Be strong in the Lord
and in His mighty Power.
Ephesians 6:10

Heal the world. Make it a better place for you and for me and the entire human race. There are people dying. If you care enough for the living, make a better place for you and for me. And the dream we were conceived in will reveal a joyful face. And the world we once believed in will shine again in grace. Then why do we keep strangling life, wound this earth, crucify it soul? It's plain to see this world is heavenly. Be God's glow.
Heal The World (Michael Jackson)

So, let's not allow ourselves to get fatigued doing good. At the right time we will harvest a good crop if we don't give up, or quit. Right now, therefore, every time we get the chance, let us work for the benefit of all.
Galatians 6:9-10a (MSG)

Journaling Prompt:
The world can sometimes feel so broken and hard. What can you do to make a positive impact?

_____
_____
_____
_____
_____
_____
_____
_____
_____
_____
_____
_____
_____
_____
_____
_____
_____
_____
_____
_____
_____
_____
_____
_____
_____
_____
_____

You raise me up, so I can stand on mountains.
You raise me up to walk on stormy seas.
I am strong when I am on your shoulders.
You raise me up to more than I can be.
You Raise Me Up (Josh Groban)

The Lord sustains all who fall and
raises up all who are bowed down.
Psalm 145:14 (NASB)

Journaling Prompt:
In what area(s) do you sense
God raising you up?

_____
_____
_____
_____
_____
_____
_____
_____
_____
_____
_____
_____
_____
_____
_____
_____
_____
_____
_____
_____
_____
_____
_____
_____
_____
_____
_____
_____
_____
_____
_____
_____
_____
_____

There can be miracles when you believe.
Though hope is frail, it's hard to kill.
Who knows what miracles you can achieve.
When you believe, somehow you will.
You will when you believe.
When You Believe (Mariah Carey)

But I will keep hope alive, and my praise to
You will grow exponentially. I will bear witness
to Your merciful acts throughout the day. I will
speak of all the ways You deliver, although,
I admit, I do not know the entirety of either.
Psalm 71:14-15 (Voice)

Journaling Prompt:
Write about merciful acts you have observed recently and your response?

You've got a friend in me. When the road looks rough ahead and you're miles and miles. From your nice warm bed you just remember what your old pal said. You've got a friend in me. If you've got troubles, I've got 'em too. There isn't anything I wouldn't do for you. We stick together and can see it through because you've got a friend in me.
You've Got A Friend In Me (Randy Newman)

Every time you cross my mind, I break out in exclamations of thanks to God. Each exclamation is a trigger to prayer. I find myself praying for you with a glad heart.
Philippians 1:3-4 (MSG)

Journaling Prompt: For whom should I pray today? Why?

've got a river of living water, a fountain that never will run dry. It's an open Heavens You're releasing and we will never be denied. We're stirring up deep wells. We're stirring up deep waters. We're going to dance in the river. We're going to jump in the river. Deep cries out to deep cries out to You. We're falling into deeper waters, calling out to You. Deep Cries Out To Deep (Bethel Music)

God's wisdom is something mysterious that goes deep into the interior of his purposes. You don't find it lying around on the surface. It's not the latest message, but more like the oldest—what God determined as the way to bring out his best in us, long before we ever arrived on the scene.
1 Corinthians 2: 7-8 (MSG)

Journaling Prompt:
Respond: I feel you pulling me into ___ and it feels ___.

Praying Forward

FEED MY SOUL

FEED MY MIND

FEED MY BODY

FEED OTHERS

Meeting with the CEO

SCRIPTURE PASSAGE

MAIN IDEAS

ACTION ITEMS

Meeting with the CEO

SCRIPTURE PASSAGE

MAIN IDEAS

ACTION ITEMS

AND WE KNOW THAT IN ALL THINGS GOD WORKS FOR THE GOOD OF THOSE WHO LOVE HIM ROM 8:28

And we know that in all things
God works for the good of those
who love Him. Romans 8:28

SECTIONS NINE & TEN

COLORFUL MUSICAL PRAYERS

Lift up a song and strike the tambourine.

Psalm 81:2

Like peering through a window blurred with rain, emotions run together in a flood of doubt and shame. You prayed as best you can. Now you leave it in His hands. For I know if my eyes fail to see, He is able. And even though it seems impossible to me. He is able. And if He chooses not to move in the way we prayed He would, confident He's working all together for my good, I will stand behind His Word for He is able.

He Is Able (Wintley Phelps)

Now to him who is able to do immeasurably more than all we ask or imagine, according to his power that is at work within us.
Ephesians 3:20 (NLT)

Journaling Prompt:
Respond: Lord, do I dare believe You are able to ___?

Paint yourself a picture of what you wish you looked like. Maybe then they just might feel an ounce of your pain. Come into focus, step out of the shadows. It's a losing battle. There's no need to be ashamed 'cause they don't even know you. All they see is scars. They don't see the angel living in your heart. Let them find the real you buried deep within. Let them know with all you've got that you are not your skin.
Skin (Sixx A.M.)

The Spirit of God has made me, and the breath of the Almighty gives me life.
Job 33:4 (ESV)

Journaling Prompt:
Write to the angel within you.

_____
_____
_____
_____
_____
_____
_____
_____
_____
_____
_____
_____
_____
_____
_____
_____
_____
_____
_____
_____
_____
_____
_____
_____
_____
_____
_____
_____
_____
_____
_____

I heard Him say He brought me from a mighty long way. And now today, I can testify that I believe it. And on my way I realized He's the one who kept me. When the storms of life arise, sleepless nights and desperate cries. He has captured every tear assuring me He hears every prayer. Waiting on the answer only to discover He is near and He hears every prayer. He has done great things and I believe He's a God who always answers prayer.
Every Prayer (Israel Houghton)

You keep track if all my sorrows. You have collected all my tears in Your bottle. You have recorded each one in Your book.
Psalm 56:8 (NLT)

Journaling Prompt:
What difference does it make to know God sees and keeps track of all of your sorrows?

_____
_____
_____
_____
_____
_____
_____
_____
_____
_____
_____
_____
_____
_____
_____
_____
_____
_____
_____
_____
_____
_____
_____
_____
_____
_____
_____
_____
_____
_____

You call me out upon the waters; the great unknown where feet may fail. And there I find You in the mystery. in oceans deep, my faith will stand. And I will call upon Your name and keep my eyes above the waves. When oceans rise, my soul will rest in Your embrace for I am Yours and You are mine.
Oceans (Where Feet May Fail) (Hillsong United)

Peter, suddenly bold, said, "Master, if it's really you, call me to come to you on the water." He said, "Come ahead." Jumping out of the boat, Peter walked on the water to Jesus.
Matthew 14:28-29 (MSG)

Journaling Prompt:
God, help me to walk on these troubled waters.

I was running and you found me. I was blinded and you gave me sight. You put a song of praise in me. I was broken and you healed me. I was dying and you gave me life. Lord you are my identity. And I know I am forgiven. I am your friend. I am accepted. I know who I am. I am secured. I'm confident. I am loved. I know who I am. I am alive. I've been set free. I belong to you and you belong to me.
I know who I am (Israel Houghton)

I no longer call you servants, because a servant does not know his master's business. Instead, I have called you friends, John 15:15ab (NIV)

Journaling Prompt:
What difference might it make in your life if you really believe God calls you friend?

_____
_____
_____
_____
_____
_____
_____
_____
_____
_____
_____
_____
_____
_____
_____
_____
_____
_____
_____
_____
_____
_____
_____
_____
_____
_____
_____
_____
_____

Praying
Forward

FEED MY SOUL

FEED MY MIND

FEED MY BODY

FEED OTHERS

Meeting with the CEO

SCRIPTURE PASSAGE	MAIN IDEAS

ACTION ITEMS

Meeting with the CEO

SCRIPTURE PASSAGE

MAIN IDEAS

ACTION ITEMS

Doodles to *Clarity*

1 PETER 5:7 † CAST ALL YOUR CARES ON GOD BECAUSE GOD CARES FOR YOU

Cast all your cares on God because
God cares for you. 1 Peter 5:7

Lord, I hunger for holiness. And I thirst for the righteousness that's Yours. That my mind would be cleansed and my spirit renewed and this temple that You dwell in would be pure.
Hunger For Holiness (Helen Baylor)

Blessed are those who hunger and thirst for righteousness, for they shall be satisfied.
Matthew 5:6 (NIV)

Journaling Prompt:
Respond: God, I want to be satisfied. Help me _____.

_____
_____
_____
_____
_____
_____
_____
_____
_____
_____
_____
_____
_____
_____
_____
_____
_____
_____
_____
_____
_____
_____
_____
_____
_____
_____
_____
_____
_____
_____

Lord, prepare me to be a sanctuary,
pure and holy, tried and true. And with
thanksgiving, I'll be a living sanctuary for you.
Prepare Me To Be A Sanctuary (Brent Miller)

Don't you know that you yourselves
are God's temple and that
God's Spirit dwells in your midst?
1 Corinthians 3:16 (NLT)

Journaling Prompt:
What does being God's temple mean to you?

Jehovah Jireh, my provider, You are more than enough for me. Jehovah Rapha, You're my healer. By Your stripes, I have been set free. Jehovah Shamma, You are with me and You supply all of my needs. You are more than enough for me.
More Thank Enough (Brooklyn Tabernacle)

And this same God… will supply all your needs from his glorious riches, which have been given to us in Christ Jesus.
Philippians 4:19 (NLT)

Journaling Prompt:
Which name/characteristic of God (healer, provider, present) do you most need to tap into today?

_____
_____
_____
_____
_____
_____
_____
_____
_____
_____
_____
_____
_____
_____
_____
_____
_____
_____
_____
_____
_____
_____
_____
_____
_____
_____
_____
_____
_____
_____

Righteousness is what I long for. Righteousness is what I need. Righteousness is what You want from me. Holiness is what I long for. Brokenness is what I long for. Take my heart and mold it. Take my mind; transform it. Take my will; conform it to Yours, Oh Lord.
Holiness Is What I Long For (Donnie McClurken)

Don't copy the behavior and customs of this world, but let God transform you into a new person by changing the way you think. Then you will learn to know God's will for you, which is good and pleasing and perfect.
Romans 12:2 (NLT)

Journaling Prompt:
Lord, my thinking often takes me in circles. Help me ____.

Butterfly, you can do most anything your heart desires. Freedom comes with understanding who you are. It's time to reclaim your place amongst the stars. Spread your wings and fly.
Black Butterfly (Sounds Of Blackness)

For the Lord will be your confidence and will keep your foot from being caught.
Proverbs 3:26

Journaling Prompt:
How can the things you believe are holding you back be used to catapult you into your dreams?

FEED MY SOUL

FEED MY MIND

FEED MY BODY

FEED OTHERS

Meeting with the CEO

SCRIPTURE PASSAGE

MAIN IDEAS

ACTION ITEMS

Meeting with the CEO

SCRIPTURE PASSAGE	MAIN IDEAS

ACTION ITEMS

Doodles to
Clarity

Doodles to
Clarity

May the meditation of my heart
be pleasing in Your sight, O Lord,
my Rock. Psalm 19:14

BULLET PRAYERS

Power Position

Bullet Prayers

PRAYERS	UPDATES

Bullet Prayers

PRAYERS	UPDATES

Bullet Prayers

PRAYERS	UPDATES

Bullet Prayers

PRAYERS	UPDATES

Bullet Prayers

PRAYERS	UPDATES

Bullet Prayers

PRAYERS	UPDATES

Bullet Prayers

PRAYERS	UPDATES

Bullet Prayers

PRAYERS	UPDATES

Bullet Prayers

PRAYERS	UPDATES

Bullet Prayers

PRAYERS	UPDATES

Bullet Prayers

PRAYERS	UPDATES

Bullet Prayers

PRAYERS	UPDATES

Bullet Prayers

PRAYERS	UPDATES

Bullet Prayers

PRAYERS	UPDATES

Bullet Prayers

PRAYERS	UPDATES

Bullet Prayers

PRAYERS	UPDATES

Bullet Prayers

PRAYERS	UPDATES

Bullet Prayers

PRAYERS	UPDATES

Bullet Prayers

PRAYERS	UPDATES

Bullet Prayers

PRAYERS	UPDATES

Bullet Prayers

PRAYERS	UPDATES

Bullet Prayers

PRAYERS	UPDATES

Bullet Prayers

PRAYERS	UPDATES

Bullet Prayers

PRAYERS	UPDATES

Rev. Dr. Donna Cox, Pastor-at-Large, believes it is her mission to empower people to apply Biblical truths to 21st century issues in practical, transformative ways. She is a graduate of Washington University in St. Louis where she earned both the Ph.D. and M.M. degrees in Performance Practices: Choral Conducting. She earned the Masters of Theological Studies from the University of Dayton.

Dr. Cox has ministered, performed, studied and taught in various parts of the world including Glasgow, Scotland, Cuddesdon, England, Dublin, Ireland, Rome, Fossano and Florence, Italy, Ghana, West Africa, Prague, Czech Republic, Porto Alegre, Brazil and Honolulu, Hawaii.

She is the founder and Pastor-At-Large of Doxology Ministries International, Inc., a 501c3 non-denominational ministry formed to take the transformative gospel to the world! Her heart's desire is to reach women and the 20-30 Somethings. In 2009, she introduced Sabbath Rest Retreats: For Busy Women Who Need A Break. The retreats instruct women in the importance of learning to 'come apart' and to sit quietly before the God who loves them.

REV. DR. DONNA M. COX

Rev. Cox has been involved in church ministry for over thirty-five years serving a variety of denominations in various capacities from Minister of Music, Choral-Director at-Large, Marriage Builders ministry leader, Associate Minister and home group leader. In addition to being a tenured Professor of Music at the University of Dayton (OH), she serves as Interim Campus Minister for Interdenominational Ministry.
Rev. Cox is ordained by the American Baptist Churches USA.

DONNACOX
MINISTRIES

Photograph by J Renee Creations Photography

Other works from the mind & heart of Rev. Dr. Donna M. Cox

- Hezekiah Loves Music: A Sacred Adventure including a bonus book, Singing The Scriptures
- Hezekiah Loves Music: Learning Rhythms the Food Way
- The Performance Series: Anthology of Art Songs and Spirituals By Contemporary African American Composers (co-edited with Dr. Kathy M. Bullock)
- No Longer Afraid: Laying Aside The Weights of Fear and Anxiety
- Angels Encamped About Me: Provision In The Wilderness
- Integrating Music Into The Core Curriculum
- Gospel Songs Your Choir Will Love To Sing

Available at online book distributors or https://revdonc.wordpress.com/bookstore

www.ingramcontent.com/pod-product-compliance
Lightning Source LLC
Chambersburg PA
CBHW050013090426

42734CB00020B/3257